9150A

W9-CNU-983

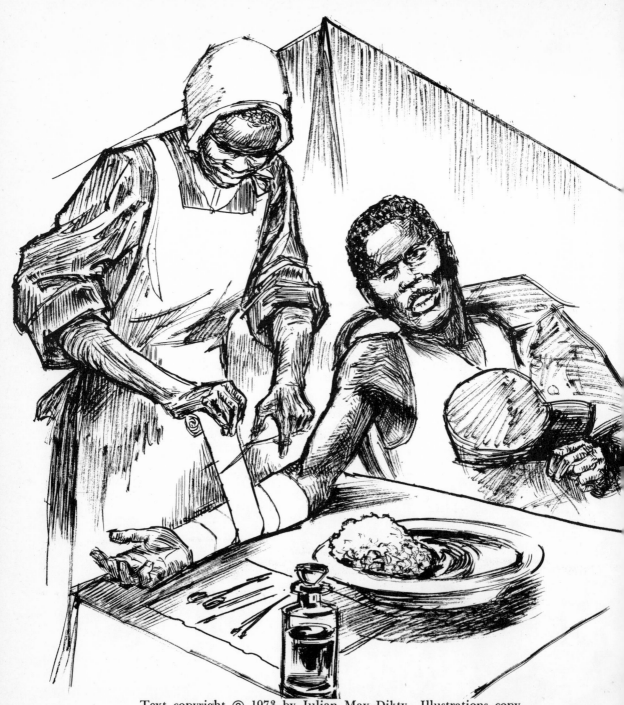

ISBN: 0-87191-228-7
Library of Congress Catalog Card Number: 72-85044

SOJOURNER TRUTH
FREEDOM-FIGHTER

Julian May

Illustrated by PHERO THOMAS

Distributed Exclusively by
CHILDRENS PRESS, CHICAGO

CREATIVE EDUCATIONAL SOCIETY, Inc.
Mankato, Minnesota 56001

SOJOURNER TRUTH

Stone Ridge Farm was crowded with people. Its master, Charles Hardenbergh, had died. And his livestock and slaves were to be sold at auction.

A skinny black girl, eleven years old, stood trembling beside her mother.

"I don't want to leave you, Ma-Ma! What if they beat me? Why can't I go free like you and Baumfree?"

"Hush, Belle," said the mother. She spoke Dutch, the language of her late master.

Old Baumfree, the girl's father, said: "Nobody would buy a broken-down old horse like me. But the law says Old Master's kin have to take care of me. So they're going to let both me and Ma-Ma Betts go free to get rid of me."

"But not me," said Belle bitterly.

Ma-Ma Betts had tears in her eyes. "No child, not you. All our other children were sold. Now it's your turn, and your little brother's."

"Just remember to obey and work hard," Baumfree said.

Ma-Ma added: "And if you pray to God, he'll see that you're treated right."

A white man came and beckoned to Belle. It was time. She said: "Good-bye, Ma-Ma. Good-bye, Baumfree."

And then she went off to be sold.

Belle's new master was John Neely. He was starting a new store near Kingston, New York. In that year of 1808, most of the settlers in the area were Dutch. Neely was not. He and his wife soon discovered that their new slavegirl could not speak a word of English. So they beat her to try to make her understand.

Afterwards, Belle would creep off into the woods and complain to God.

"Was it right for them to beat me, God? You know I'm doing the best I can. You've got to get me a new master. You have to help me, God."

But it was not until nearly a year later that help came. A jolly tavern-keeper named Schryver bought her for $105. He was Dutch and understood Belle well enough.

"You come along with me, girl," he said kindly. "If you work hard, everything will go well for you."

Belle was sure that God had answered her prayer. The tavern was an exciting place, full of guests from all over New York state. They brought gossip and news. Belle heard that the slaves in New York were going to be freed in a few years.

Freedom! What would it be like? Baumfree and Ma-Ma Betts were free—living in misery in a tiny cabin without enough food to eat or clothes to keep them warm. Was that what freedom meant?

Belle had plenty to eat at the Schryver's place. She grew six feet tall by the time she was 13 years old. In winter, she had a warm shawl. And she even had shoes—a cast-off pair of the master's because women's shoes were too small for her feet.

Life was so good that she almost forgot how to pray.

In 1810, when Belle was 13, she was sold to a wealthy man named John Dumont. He was the handsomest man Belle had ever seen. "God must look like that!" she thought.

Dumont was very kind to Belle. The other slaves and the white servant-girl, Katie, were jealous. Then one day Dumont exclaimed: "Look at these potatoes you cooked, Belle. They are full of dirt." And he whipped her.

The blows did not hurt much. But Belle had begun to love John Dumont and wanted to please him.

Dumont's little daughter wanted to help Belle. She said, "I'll watch the potatoes for you as they cook."

Dumont's daughter saw the servant, Katie, creep up and throw ashes into the pot. When Dumont found out the truth about the dirty potatoes he punished Katie and smiled at Belle.

"I always knew you were a good girl," he said.

And Belle loved him more than ever.

As the years passed, there were always rumors of freedom. She thought: "When I'm free, I'll go and take care of Baumfree and Ma-Ma."

But her mother died not long after she came to the Dumonts'. And after that, there was no one to care for blind, crippled Baumfree. He died of hunger and cold in his lonely cabin in the forest.

Dumont allowed Belle to go to his funeral. She saw that the Hardenbergh family had sent a fine coffin for the burial of their faithful old slave.

Belle cried out to the sky: "What good is a nice box to put him in? God, why didn't they help him when he was alive and hurting? God, why didn't you set me free in time to help him?"

In 1817, Belle was married to a slave named Tom. That same year, the New York legislature passed a law to free all the slaves in ten years' time.

It seemed a long way off.

Meanwhile, Belle remained with the Dumonts, her master's favorite. She had at least four children. Some of the slaves whispered that the children seemed too light-colored to be the offspring of old Tom. Belle paid no attention to them. They were just jealous because she was treated so well. Her master was the kindest person in the world and she repaid him by working harder than any of the others.

And then, two years before the slaves were to go free, John Dumont decided to sell Belle's five-year-old son, a lovable boy named Peter.

Belle was struck with horror. "Don't do it, Master! Don't sell my boy! What if they beat him? What if they send him down South where he'll *never* be free?"

Dumont laughed. "Peter is going to live with my friend, Dr. Gedney. He'll learn nice manners and live in the big house. Why—he'll be like a pet!"

But Belle would not be comforted. Finally Dumont said that he would give her her freedom a year early if she just stopped complaining. Weeping, Belle agreed.

The year went by. Then Belle reminded her kind master of his promise. But he refused to let her go. "I need you for another year," he said.

Belle went off and prayed. "God, you have to tell me what to do!" And the answer came to her: *Go away.*

She said: "God, I'm afraid to go at night. But if I go in daytime, somebody will see me."

Again the answer came: *Go at dawn.*

So she took her baby, Sophia, and a bundle with food and clothes. Just as gray light showed in the east, she walked away from the Dumont estate.

"I'm on my way, God," she said. "But you better show me where to go."

Belle found shelter in the home of a Quaker couple, Isaac and Maria Van Wagener. These good people believed that slavery was wrong and promised to hire her for a small salary. But before many hours had passed, there was a pounding at the door.

It was Dumont. He said, calmly, "Well, Belle, so you've run away."

She said: "No, Master, I walked away. You promised me that I would be free."

"You must come back."

But she said, firmly: "No, Master. I won't."

"Then I'll take the child," Dumont said, reaching for little Sophia.

Isaac Van Wagener came forward with a purse of money. "I do not believe in buying and selling human beings," he said. "But I will buy Belle's services for one year, and those of the baby as well. After that, as you know, she will be free by law."

Dumont finally agreed to accept $25. Then he turned, mounted his horse, and rode away.

Belle turned to Van Wagener. "I'll serve you well, Master."

"There is only one Master of mankind," the Quaker said with a smile. "And now, if you wish, you may go to work."

In the weeks that followed, Belle worked for the Van Wageners and slowly began to "grow up." She was nearly 30 years old. But for most of her life she had been treated like a child. It took time for her to learn to know her own mind—to realize what freedom really meant.

On July 4, 1827, Belle and all the other New York slaves became officially free. It was a happy day. But not long after, Belle had news that filled her full of fear and anger.

The Gedneys had sent her son, little Peter, to Alabama. As long as he stayed there, he would not be free.

"What they have done is against the law!" declared old Isaac Van Wagener.

A light came into Belle's tear-filled eyes. "If that's so," she said, "then I'll have my child again!" And she ran out the front door, straight to the Gedney farm.

There she screamed: "I'll have my child again!"

Old Mrs. Gedney came out and looked at her coldly. She said: "My daughter, Liza, has married John Fowler and taken Peter to serve her in Alabama. We have *both* lost our dear children. Now go away at once."

She went off, weeping. "God, show them that you're my helper. Please help me!"

A stranger came up to her in the road. He said: "Go up to that house and tell them your story." She went.

The people who welcomed her were Quakers, like the Van Wageners, and strongly opposed to slavery. They said: "Tomorrow we will send you to the county courthouse at Kingston. If you tell your story to the grand jury, you may be able to get your son back."

The next day, Belle went off to test the power of the law. She made a lawyer listen to her story. He gave her a writ, a court order, to send to the Gedneys. If the man who had sold the boy did not bring him back, he could go to prison. Belle settled down to wait.

Some time passed and the whole valley talked about the amazing thing that Belle had done. An ex-slave taking a rich white man to law! What were the times coming to?

Little Peter was brought back. And to Belle's great joy, the judge handed him over to her. "Praise God!" said Belle. Later, when she undressed Peter for bed, she saw that his little back was scarred from terrible beatings.

"My poor boy!" she said. "Who did this?"

"Master Fowler," Peter said. "He whip Miz Eliza, too. He whip just about *ever*body."

A terrible hatred filled Belle. She whispered a curse: "O Lord, render unto them double!"

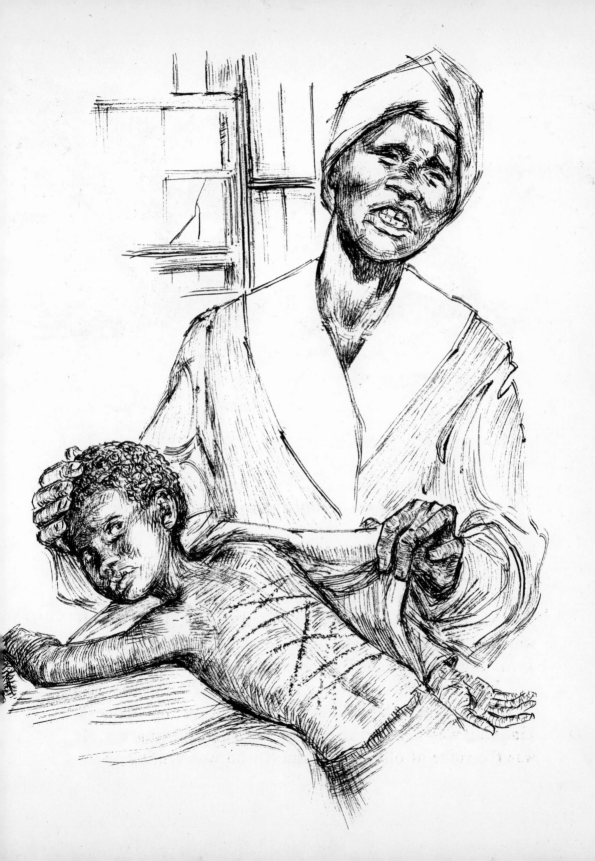

Freedom for a slave brought many problems. Belle was often lonesome for the company of black people as she did her quiet housework. She began to forget the bad parts of slavery and remember only the secure feeling of being taken care of—of not having to think for herself.

Most of all, she missed her kind master, Dumont. It was true that the Bible said that her love for him had been a sin. But he was so handsome and kind!

Belle still had not grown up.

That winter, she worked for a cousin of the Gedneys. Hanging wash in the yard, she heard a scream ring out. It was the voice of old Mrs. Gedney, who was visiting.

"Eliza!" the old lady shrieked. "My daughter!"

Belle crept inside to listen. She heard the old lady reading aloud from a letter. "Fowler has gone insane and has murdered poor Eliza. . . ."

Render unto them double.

"O no, God!" said Belle. "I didn't mean quite so much! Forgive me, God. I didn't mean it!"

She fled back to the Van Wagener house and wept for days. She felt alone, and very guilty.

A few days later, there was a knock at the door. John Dumont stood there, smiling. "I've come to take you back, Belle," he said. And he beckoned her to follow him.

"Yes, Master!" she said happily. She took her baby and started to follow.

In later years, she tried to describe what happened to her next. It was like an invisible arm—strong, so strong—and a mighty voice saying: *Not another step.*

Dumont turned to look at her in amazement. She did not move and could not speak. At last he shook his head and drove away. Maria Van Wagener laid a hand on Belle's arm.

"What is the matter, Belle?"

"I saw—God give me such a look!"

"You saw *God?*" exclaimed the old lady.

Belle whispered: "I didn't know God was so big. He's all over."

It was a turning point in her life. Never again did she long for slavery, for the childish comfort of a human master. Now there would be only one Master for her.

For many days she thought about what had happened to her. She felt a great love rise in her heart to replace the burnt-out hate.

"Lord, I can even love the white folks!" she cried.

Belle worked in upstate New York until 1829. Then a kind woman named Miss Geer invited her to come to New York City, where the wages were higher.

The city was in a turmoil. There were thousands of freed slaves without work and many penniless Irish immigrants as well, all living in stinking slums. Miss Geer joined a group of street preachers that went out and tried to bring the word of God to the poor. Before too long, Belle began to help. Because she was black and as tall as a man, she was able to protect the white ladies as they went through the dark, dangerous streets.

Belle learned many parts of the Bible by heart. She was growing up fast now, and her excellent mind was making up for the empty slave years. Now and then she tried a bit of preaching herself. She was amazed that her words were able to stir the hearts of others.

Years went by. Anti-slavery feeling was stronger and stronger in the land. Leaders called abolitionists made speeches against slavery, staged demonstrations, and wrote fiery articles. Ordinary people of all kinds felt a new kind of religious power rising within them. All over New England there were outdoor religious meetings, called camp meetings, where people gathered to pray, sing, and hear preaching about black freedom, the rights of women, and many other strange, new things.

Belle herself had to wait until 1843 before receiving another divine message. Then, one summer morning, she seemed to hear a voice saying: *Leave the city and go east.*

She got on a ferry-boat and crossed to Long Island. There she began to walk, feeling lonely and unsure of what God wanted her to do.

She remembered a Bible verse: *Hear my prayer, O Lord . . . for I am a stranger with thee and a sojourner, as all my fathers were.*

Her fathers had come from Africa to this strange land of white people. Here they were sold, separated from relatives and friends. They were all sojourners—travelers never finding a true home.

An idea came to her. She would cast away her "slave name" of Isabelle and take a new one. And she would pick a last name, too. Only slaves had no last name.

Another Bible verse came to her: *You shall know the truth, and the truth shall make you free.*

The next day, she came up to a camp meeting. "I want to speak!" she said. "God has sent me. My name is Sojourner Truth."

The people did not dare to laugh at her. She stood before them and told them of her life as a slave—the cruelty, the horror of being sold or having your own children sold. The middle-class people at the meeting had never owned slaves. Many of them wept softly as she told them what had happened to Peter.

Sojourner Truth was an instant success as a preacher. She traveled from meeting to meeting, speaking and singing hymns in her rich, deep voice. There were always friends to give her shelter, food, and other necessities.

One evening, she was to speak at a meeting in Connecticut. A mob of young men who were in favor of slavery came to set the tents on fire and break up the service.

Sojourner went out alone to face the hoodlums. She began to sing a hymn and the gang rushed at her with clubs.

"Why do you come at me with sticks?" she scolded. "I'm doing no harm."

They began to laugh and mock her. "Keep singing, old woman! Say a prayer for us!"

She began to preach for them. Slowly, the laughing stopped. The clubs were laid down. She spoke of God's love for all mankind for nearly an hour and the mob of toughs listened.

"Now I'll sing you one more hymn, and then you'll go," she said firmly. The music of her voice filled the night. And when it was over, the mob melted slowly away.

She was the first black woman to preach against slavery. Some abolitionists of that time were also champions of women's rights. Sojourner Truth took up this cause, too. Often pro-slavery people in the audience would heckle her.

One man shouted: "Old woman, who cares what you say? Your chatter is no more to me than a flea-bite!"

She said: "Maybe not. But the good Lord willing, I'll keep you scratching!"

In the year 1850, a friend named Olive Gilbert helped Sojourner write a little book. It was called THE NARRATIVE OF SOJOURNER TRUTH, A NORTHERN SLAVE. She sold the book wherever she made her speeches. Famous anti-slavery speakers such as Wendell Phillips and William Lloyd Garrison became her friends.

At a convention of the Anti-Slavery Society, she listened to the famous black abolitionist, Frederick Douglass. His voice was full of despair as he described the evils inflicted on the black race by the white.

"It must come to blood!" Douglass cried. "Black men must fight. They have no other hope."

No other hope? Sojourner Truth rose up to confront her fellow freedom-fighter. *No* other hope?

"Frederick," she asked, "is God dead?"

Frederick Douglass' words came true in the end. The question of slavery was only answered in blood. Lincoln became President. The South seceded from the Union. The Civil War began in 1861.

Sojourner now made her home in the Middle West, where she felt she could do the most for the cause of freedom. Even though she was now an old woman, she traveled from place to place giving abolitionist speeches. At times, mobs threatened her life. She was often arrested. A severe beating by hoodlums left her partly crippled.

Still, she continued to speak. Her people were not yet free.

During the first part of the war, Lincoln fought to save the Union rather than to free the slaves. But later, with the North losing battle after battle, he made a proclamation: If the South did not lay down its arms, he would declare all southern slaves to be forever free.

The South fought on. And Lincoln issued the Emancipation Proclamation on January 1, 1863.

When Sojourner received the news, she was sick in bed. But suddenly she knew she could no longer "afford" to be ill. She got up and began to work again, cooking warm meals for the black troops that were stationed nearby.

Then she felt she had to see the President, the man who had set her people free. Friends brought her to the White House and introduced her to Abraham Lincoln.

The President took her hand and bowed. "I'm pleased to see you," he said.

Sojourner said: "Mr. Lincoln, I never heard tell of you before they put you up for president!"

Lincoln's eyes twinkled. "But I had heard of you," he said. For a few more minutes they talked. He showed her a splendid Bible, presented to him by the ex-slaves of Baltimore. Then he signed his name in a little book she had brought: *For Aunty Sojourner Truth, October 29, 1864. A. Lincoln.*

"I hope we will meet again," the President said.

Sojourner Truth went to work at Freedmen's Village, near Washington. She was a teacher and friend to the often bewildered ex-slaves. When the war ended, she rejoiced with them. When Lincoln was killed, she calmed their fears that they would lose their freedom. As a last great task, she tried to make Congress grant western land to freed slaves.

Congress would not act. But by 1879, thousands of black families had gone West by themselves. Sojourner Truth went to Kansas to welcome them and help them get settled.

Her work done, she retired to her home in Battle Creek, Michigan. There she died on November 6, 1883. On her gravestone they carved:

IN MEMORIAM — SOJOURNER TRUTH
"IS GOD DEAD?"